*STYLE IT: TRENDS AND FADS

Jewelry Joy

by VIRGINIA LOH-HAGAN

45TH PARALLEL PRESS

Published in the United States of America by
Cherry Lake Publishing Group
Ann Arbor, Michigan
www.cherrylakepublishing.com

Reading Adviser: Beth Walker Gambro, MS, Ed., Reading Consultant, Yorkville, IL
Book Designer: Joseph Hatch

Photo Credits: rogerblake1, CC BY 2.0 via Flickr, cover; © Max kegfire/Shutterstock, 4;
© nata_nytiaga/Shutterstock, 7; Livrustkammaren (The Royal Armoury) / Erik Lernestål /
CC BY-SA, Public domain, via Wikimedia Commons, 8; Public Domain via Wikimedia
Commons, 11; Hallwyl Museum, Public domain, via Wikimedia Commons, 13; Image courtesy
of Chari Cuthbert, BYCHARI Jewelry, 14; John Jabez Edwin Mayall, Public domain,
via Wikimedia Commons, 16; Jacob/Pexels.com, 19; Oks Malkova/Pexels.com, 21;
© EgolenaHK/Shutterstock, 22; © EyeEm Mobile GmbH/iStock, 24; © designkida/
Shutterstock, 27; © DuxX/Shutterstock, 28; © Shiiko Alexander/Shutterstock, 31

Copyright © 2026 by Cherry Lake Publishing Group

All rights reserved. No part of this book may be reproduced or utilized in any form
or by any means without written permission from the publisher.

45th Parallel Press is an imprint of Cherry Lake Publishing Group.

Library of Congress Cataloging-in-Publication Data has been filed and is available
at catalog.loc.gov

Cherry Lake Publishing Group would like to acknowledge the work of the Partnership
for 21st Century Learning, a Network of Battelle for Kids. Please visit Battelle for Kids
online for more information.

Note from publisher: Websites change regularly, and their future contents are outside
of our control. Supervise children when conducting any recommended online searches
for extended learning opportunities.

Printed in the United States of America

Dr. Virginia Loh-Hagan is an author and educator. She is currently the Executive
Director for Asian American Native Hawaiian Pacific Islander Affairs at San Diego
State University and the Co-Executive Director of The Asian American Education
Project. She lives in San Diego with her very tall husband and very naughty dogs.

TABLE *of CONTENTS

INTRODUCTION 5

CHAPTER 1: **Bezoar Jewelry** 9

CHAPTER 2: **Jewel Beetle Wings** 10

CHAPTER 3: **Ambergris Pomanders** 12

CHAPTER 4: **Lovers' Eyes** 15

CHAPTER 5: **Hair Jewelry**......................17

CHAPTER 6: **Chameleon Jewelry**............18

CHAPTER 7: **Feet Jewelry** 20

CHAPTER 8: **Memorial Diamonds**.......... 23

CHAPTER 9: **Permanent Jewelry** 25

CHAPTER 10: **Smart Jewelry** 26

DO YOUR PART! 29

GLOSSARY... 32

LEARN MORE 32

INDEX.. 32

There are always new jewelry trends!
Which ones have you seen lately?

INTRODUCTION

Everybody has style. Some people have more style than others. They stand out. They use **fashion** to express themselves. Fashion is about how people want to look. It's about how people dress. It includes clothes, shoes, hats, and jewelry. It also includes hairstyles and makeup.

Fashion changes across cultures. It changes over time. There are many fashion **trends**. Trends are fads. They're patterns of change. They reflect what's popular at a certain time. Many people copy popular looks. They copy famous people. They get inspired. They want to be cool. They want to be in style.

Some trends last a long time. Other trends are short. All trends make history.

Pieces of jewelry are personal ornaments. They adorn the body. They include necklaces. They include rings. They include bracelets. They're made from jewels. They're made from metals. They can be made from anything.

People wear jewelry for different reasons. Married people may wear wedding rings. Some people use jewelry to express themselves. Some use it to enhance how they look. Jewelry adds beauty. It adds personality. It signals one's role in society. It plays a key role in fashion.

Some jewelry is big. Some is small. Some is bold. Some is simple. There have been a lot of jewelry trends. This book features some of the fun ones!

Some jewelry is passed down. It holds special memories.

This bezoar ring was made for Hedvig Eleonora of Hostein-Gottorp (1632–1715).
She was the queen of Sweden.

CHAPTER

One

Bezoar Jewelry

Bezoars collect in the stomach. Bezoars are balls or clumps. They look like stones. Hair and other things might not pass through the body. Instead, they form bezoars. Some people believed bezoars had healing powers. Bezoars became more valuable than gold.

Bezoar jewelry started in the Middle East in the first century. Bezoars could be found in animals. They were turned into jewelry charms. They were set into rings. They were worn as **pendants**. Pendants hang from a chain. People thought wearing bezoars protected them from poisons.

Bezoar jewelry came back in the 12th century. Europe was suffering from the Black **Plague**. Plagues are deadly illnesses that spread quickly.

CHAPTER TWO

Jewel Beetle Wings

Elytra are hard beetle wings. These wings are in the front. They're not used for flight. They protect the beetle's soft body and wings. Jewel beetles are large. They have beautiful wings. Their wings are shiny. They're colorful. They look like jewels. They have been used in fashion.

People in South America and Asia use jewel beetles. This practice was popular in India from 1526 to 1857. Elytra were used whole. They were cut up into parts. They were sewn into jewelry and clothes. Gold thread was often used. Such art signaled high class.

Great Britain invaded India. Their rule lasted from 1858 to 1947. They liked the elytra designs. They brought this practice to Europe.

FASHION-FORWARD PIONEER

Johnny Dang is Vietnamese American. His family left Vietnam in 1987. They moved to Houston, Texas. Dang's father and grandfather worked in the jewelry business. Dang started by repairing jewelry. He opened his first store in a mall. He did this in 1998. He's now known as the "king of bling." He has designed jewelry for famous rappers. He makes custom grills. Grills are worn over teeth. They're made of metal. They're part of the hip-hop scene. Dang made popular grills with jewels. He's a pioneer in dental jewelry. He has even appeared in music videos. He has been mentioned in songs.

VonRyan The Genius is a musical artist. Here, he shows his Johnny Dang & Company permanent white gold, diamond teeth.

CHAPTER

THREE

Ambergris Pomanders

Ambergris is made in the guts of sperm whales. It's solid and waxy. It's black and soft. It's smelly. But when hardened, it turns yellow. It has a sweet scent. It's been used in perfumes. It makes scents last longer.

Ancient Egyptians used ambergris necklaces. But they became popular in the Middle Ages in Europe. This period lasted from 500 to 1500. People feared getting sick.

Many wore **pomanders**. Pomanders are balls of scented materials. They had ambergris. They were attached to necklaces. They were attached to belts. People thought they protected against sickness. They thought they protected against witchcraft.

The woman in this painting holds a gold pomander.
It likely held ambergris and other scented things inside.

FASHION REBEL: Trendsetter

Chari Cuthbert designs jewelry. She taught herself. She was born in Jamaica. She now lives in California. She started her own business in 2012. Her jewelry company is called BYCHARI. When she started, she only had $100. Today, she makes jewelry for famous people. Michelle Obama was the U.S. First Lady. In 2020, she made a speech. She wore Cuthbert's necklace. The necklace had the word, "Vote." This necklace went viral. It was a top-trending search. People wanted that necklace. Cuthbert said, "I felt that as a female owner of a company, with a massive base of female customers, it was important to make my voice heard about the power of voting."

Chari Cuthbert, creator and owner of BYCHARI

Lovers' Eyes

Lovers' eyes were small paintings of eyes on ivory. They showed the eyes of loved ones. These paintings were framed. They were worn as bracelets, **brooches**, pendants, or rings. Brooches are jewelry with pins or clasps. They are worn around the neck area.

King George IV started the trend. He ruled Great Britain. When he was a prince, he fell in love. He had a crush on Maria Fitzherbert. Their love was banned by the court.

He wanted to send her a love token. But he didn't want to be found out. So he sent her a painting of his right eye. She sent him a painting of her eye. This happened in 1785. The fad took off. Lovers all over Europe had jewelry with eyes.

After Prince Albert died, Queen Victoria wore special jewelry to remember him. She wore only black clothes until her death.

CHAPTER

Hair Jewelry

Lockets are pendants that open. They hold things. Hair jewelry began in the Middle Ages. English soldiers had lockets. Their lockets held the hair of loved ones.

Queen Victoria began the modern hair jewelry trend. Victoria ruled Great Britain from 1837 to 1901. Her husband was Prince Albert. Albert gave her a bracelet with lockets of their children's hair. Albert died in 1861. Victoria was sad. She wore jewelry made of his hair.

Hair was a symbol of life after death. Victoria popularized **mourning** hair jewelry. Mourning is the act of grieving someone's death. She also wore black clothing for the rest of her life. She set mourning trends.

CHAPTER

SiX

Chameleon Jewelry

New York City has been a hub for fashion. It has set many trends. In the 1890s, it led the way for **chameleon** jewelry. Chameleons are small lizards. They change colors.

Thousands of chameleons were shipped from South America. Women bought them. They attached chains to their necks. Then they pinned these chains to their clothing. The chameleons changed colors to match the clothing. They became playthings.

In the 1920s, young girls put leashes on lizards. They wore them in their hair.

This trend upset animal **activists**. Activists fight for change. They want a better world. They stopped the use of live animals as jewelry.

DIY FASHION FUN

ADD SOME BLING TO YOUR LOOK. CREATE SOME SPARKLE. HERE ARE SOME IDEAS:

» Wear many pieces of jewelry at once. Stack your rings. Stack your necklaces. Combine different colors. Combine different types. Mismatch earrings. This lets you get more wear out of your jewelry. It also creates new looks with old pieces.

» Host a jewelry swap. Trade pieces with friends or families. Freshen up your closet. Get new pieces without spending more money. Make sure to ask about the history of each piece. Jewelry can have stories.

» Get thread and make friendship bracelets. Get beads and make bracelets. Give them to loved ones. There are many patterns.

CHAPTER

Feet Jewelry

Anklets are bracelets worn around ankles. Ancient Egyptian women wore anklets. Anklets showed off social class. They could be made from string, leather, or wood. For rich women, they were made from metals and gems.

Anklets emerged in the United States in the 1940s. Frank Sinatra was a popular singer. His fans were called "Bobby Soxers." **Bobby socks** are white. They end at the ankles. Some fans wore anklets to highlight their bobby socks. In the 1970s, anklets were part of the hippie vibe.

Shoe jewelry is also trending. People attach objects to their shoes. These include pins, charms, and gems. The shoes are like **miniature** art galleries. Miniature means a very small copy of something.

Today, people wear toe rings. Toe rings have a beach vibe.

Memorial Diamonds

Diamonds are valuable gems. They're most often used for rings, earrings, and necklaces. Real diamonds take billions of years to form. They need to be **mined**. This means dug from the earth.

In the 1950s, scientists made fake diamonds. They did this in a lab. In 2003, **memorial** diamonds were invented. Memorials preserve memories. These diamonds are made from human hair and ashes.

When people die, some choose to get **cremated**. Cremation means to burn to ashes. Each memorial diamond is unique. No two are alike. This is a costly process. It can take months.

People turn memorial diamonds into jewelry. They feel close to their loved ones.

> Today, diamonds are still popular. But more people are buying diamonds made in labs.

Today, getting matching tattoos is popular.
When placed together, the designs are whole.

CHAPTER

nine

Permanent Jewelry

Tattoos are body art. Ink is inserted into the skin to form an image. Tattooing has been around since ancient times. Tattoos are **permanent**. Permanent means forever.

Tattoos became popular in the United States in the 1990s. Some people have wedding ring tattoos. These are more permanent than jewelry. Tattoos can't just be taken off. Removal can be difficult. It can be expensive.

Today, another kind of permanent jewelry is trending. People pick out bracelets. They pick out necklaces. They wear this jewelry all the time.

Jewelers use a special tool. They fit the jewelry to the person. They **weld** the metal at the part where a clasp would be. Weld means to melt metal to join it together. Permanent jewelry can't easily be taken off.

CHAPTER

Smart Jewelry

Today, people wear their technology. Smart jewelry has sensors. It has wireless charging. It has small displays. It can perform many functions. There are many types of smart jewelry. They include rings, bracelets, and watches.

The first wave of smart jewelry tracked fitness. It tracked steps. It tracked sleep. Tech got better. Safety and security smart jewelry emerged. This had tracking systems. It had alarm systems.

The recent wave of smart jewelry tracks wellness and health. It helps manage stress. The jewelry tracks heart rates.

Tech keeps changing. It keeps improving. Who knows what will be next?

Many brands make smart rings now. This one is made by Android.

Need some new jewelry? Think about animals and the environment the next time you shop!

DO YOUR PART!

It's always fashionable to stand up for what's right. Fashion can be more than just about looks. It can be used to fight for causes. Be a fashion activist. Activists fight for change. They want a better world. Here are some ways to make a difference:

- Wear only **cruelty-free** and **vegan** jewelry. Cruelty-free means no animals were harmed. Vegan means no animals were used. Avoid leather. Avoid pearls. Avoid beeswax. Avoid feathers. Avoid fur. Avoid shells. Protect animals while still wearing pretty jewelry.

- Wear gems from responsible companies. Think about how gems were mined. Think about labor rights. Think about the environment. Protect human rights.

- Wear jewelry made from recycled materials. Or make your own jewelry. Use things you already have at your house. This helps nature. It also reduces trash. Protect the planet.

- Support small businesses. Support businesses owned by women. Support businesses owned by people of color. Help people make a living.

- Know where jewelry comes from. Know the source. Some jewelry may have been stolen. Some has been taken from different cultures. Respect the original owners.

- Appreciate cultures. Don't wear cultural jewelry without knowing about the culture.

Remember, every little bit counts. Kindness matters. You can look good and feel great!

FIGHTING FOR JUSTICE

Indigenous Americans fight for their land rights.

They fight to preserve their culture. This includes their jewelry. Native jewelry is an art. It belongs to Indigenous Americans. But some people lie. They pretend to make or sell real Native jewelry. But the pieces are fake. The Indian Arts and Crafts Act (IACA) was passed in 1990. This law protects buyers from being tricked. It protects Indigenous Americans' livelihood. They have the right to make money. Edison Yazzie is a Navajo jewelry artist. Many of his designs were stolen. People sold fake knock-offs of his work. In 2015, his case went to court. It was called the *United States v. 99,337 Pieces of Counterfeit Native American Jewelry*. The fakers were punished.

Glossary

activists (AK-tih-vists) people who fight for political or social change

ambergris (AM-buhr-gris) waxy substance vomited by sperm whales and found floating on the ocean or onshore

anklets (ANG-kluhts) ornaments worn around ankles

bezoars (BEE-zohrz) masses of undigested material that collects in the guts of animals

bobby socks (BAH-bee SAHKS) white socks reaching above the ankle and usually worn by children and teen girls

brooches (BROH-chuhz) jewelry with pins or clasps, worn around the neck area

chameleon (kuh-MEEL-yuhn) a lizard that changes color

cremated (KREE-may-tuhd) disposed of human or animal remains by burning it to ashes

cruelty-free (KROOL-tee-FREE) free from animal testing

elytra (EH-luh-truh) hardened forewings of beetles that serve as protective coverings for the soft body and flight wings

fashion (FAA-shuhn) any way of dressing that is favored or popular at any one time or place

memorial (muh-MOHR-ee-uhl) object or ceremony that serves to preserve remembrance

mined (MYND) dug from the ground

miniature (MIH-nee-uh-chur) very small copy of something

mourning (MOHR-ning) expression of deep sorrow for someone who has died

pendants (PEN-duhnts) pieces of jewelry that hang from a chain worn around the neck

permanent (PUHR-muh-nuhnt) lasting forever

plague (PLAYG) deadly sickness that spreads quickly

pomanders (POH-man-duhrz) balls or containers with holes used to hold sweet-smelling substances

trends (TRENDZ) fads or changes that are popular or common

vegan (VEE-guhn) containing no animal products

weld (WELD) to melt metal in order to attach it to other metal

Learn More

Carlson-Berne, Emma. *Jewelry Tips & Tricks.* Minneapolis, MN: Lerner Publications, 2016.

Knots, Masha. *The Beginner's Guide to Friendship Bracelets: Essential Lessons for Creating Stylish Designs to Wear and Give.* San Rafael, CA: Rocky Nook, 2022.

Loh-Hagan, Virginia. *Fashion.* Ann Arbor, MI: Cherry Lake, 2021.

Wilson, Lakita. *My Cool Jewelry.* Minneapolis, MN: Lerner Publications, 2022.

Index

ambergris pomanders, 12–13
animal products, 9–10, 12, 15, 18, 29
anklets, 20–21

bezoar jewelry, 8–9
body art, 11, 24–25
bracelets, 6, 15, 17, 19, 25–26, 31
brooches, 15

chameleon jewelry, 18
cruelty-free jewelry, 29
cultural appropriation, 30–31
Cuthbert, Chari, 14

Dang, Johnny, 11
diamonds, 11, 22–23
DIY projects, 19

feet jewelry, 20–21

gems, 6–7, 11, 20, 22–23, 29
George IV, 15

hair jewelry, 9, 16–18

Indian Arts and Crafts Act (1990), 31

jewel beetle wings, 10
jewelry designers, 11, 14, 31

lockets, 17
lovers' eyes, 15

memorial diamonds, 22–23
mourning jewelry, 17

Native jewelry, 31
necklaces, 6–7, 9, 12, 14–15, 17, 25, 31

permanent jewelry, 11, 24–25

Queen Victoria, 16–17

rings, 6, 8–9, 15, 21, 25–27, 31

shoe jewelry, 20
smart jewelry, 26–27
sustainability, 19, 29–30

tattoos, 24–25
teeth, 11
toe rings, 21

vegan jewelry, 29

watches, 4, 26, 28